G A M E   **D A Y**

Also by Derek Jeter

THE LIFE YOU IMAGINE

(with Jack Curry)

MY LIFE ON
AND OFF THE FIELD

DEREK JETER

Edited by Kristin Kiser

THREE RIVERS PRESS

NEW YORK

Published by Three Rivers Press, New York, New York.
Member of the Crown Publishing Group.

Random House, Inc. New York, Toronto, London, Sydney, Auckland
www.randomhouse.co m

THREE RIVERS PRESS is a registered trademark and the Three Rivers Press colophon is a trademark of Random House, Inc.

Printed in Korea

Design by Scott Citron

Library of Congress Cataloging-in-Publication Data
Jeter, Derek, 1974– .
Game day: my life on and off the field / by Derek Jeter.—1st ed.
1. Jeter, Derek, 1974– . 2. Baseball players—United States—Biography. 3. New York Yankees (baseball team).
4. Baseball—United States. I. Title.
GV865.J48A32   2001
796.357'092—dc21   2001027784

ISBN 0-609-80794-3

10 9 8 7 6 5 4 3 2 1

First Edition

To baseball **fans** everywhere.

Acknowledgments

I want to thank my editor, Kristin Kiser, for her guidance in putting this book together, and photographer Walter Iooss, Jr., who took many of the pictures.

CONTENTS

Introduction

THERE HAVE BEEN A LOT OF GAME DAYS IN MY LIFE.
I have been playing baseball for as long as I remember. It would be impossible for me to even begin to figure out how many times I have stepped out on the baseball field, ready to play ball. As a boy in Kalamazoo, I lived for game day. When the season would start, I would put my uniform on and ask my parents how I looked. I loved the whole ritual of game day: putting on my uniform, driving to the field, doing our warm-ups, hearing the crowd cheer and my name called, and taking my place at shortstop. It's a thrilling memory, and one that I relive every time I put on a Yankee uniform today.

In this book you will get an inside look at my life as I prepare for game day as a New York Yankee. The baseball season is really divided into three parts: spring training, the regular season, and, if we play well throughout the year, the postseason. Everything we do during spring training and the regular season is done for one reason—to make it to the ultimate game days of all, the World Series.

Game day during spring training is pretty relaxed, though there is an undercurrent of seriousness to what we do. We are practicing our drills and playing games in the warm Tampa air for a reason—so that we will have a successful season. I love going to Legends Field, our facility in Tampa. It's the best in baseball, in beautiful shape. It's an exciting time when our manager, Joe Torre, and the coaches and all the players show up in Tampa after we have been apart since October. I spend so much time with these guys during the year, and I can't wait to get out on the field with them during these early practice games.

Game day during the regular season is something special if you are a New York Yankee. This is the only uniform I've ever worn, but even when you talk to players who have been on other teams, wearing the pinstripes is a unique experience that's hard to compare with anything else. There is so much tradition behind us, and our fans really appreciate that fact. So game day for the Yankees means living up to our own aspirations, to those of our fans who continue to stand by us, and to those of our predecessors, the legendary teams that have paved the way to 26 world championships and counting. This history and the fans that have always supported us make every game day special, even when we have 162 games to get through. I will never get tired of hearing the crowd cheer when we take the field at Yankee Stadium. I feel as pumped up today as I did the very first time I set foot on Yankee soil.

If everything comes together for us during the regular season and we stay healthy and play hard, then we get to the biggest game days: those in the postseason. I don't care how many times I make it to the postseason with the Yankees, I want to do it again and again. The season is a failure if we don't win the World Series. Every lap I run in spring training or catch I make in the early days of the season or home run I hit during the homestretch in August brings me to where I really want to be—at the stadium, with the roar of the crowd in my ears and hearing my name called at the World Series. This is the biggest thrill in the world.

When I hear the words "game day," more than anything I think about having fun. I am having fun during spring training, I am having fun during the regular season, and I am really having fun playing those games in September and October where everything is on the line. There are many more game days in my future—I just can't imagine life without baseball, without fun. I know I will feel this way until the very last time I take the field.

SPRING FEVER

When February rolls around every year, I feel like I am getting ready to write another chapter in a book. That's what every new baseball season feels like to me—another chapter in a book—and I guess spring training would be the first chapter. It's an exciting time for all of the players. We haven't seen one another since the end of October, and it's a great feeling to get everyone together again. Tino Martinez, our first baseman, and I live in Tampa, but the other players are spread out all over the country. When we first get to Legends Field in the spring, we are all kind of anxious, yet we somehow manage to pick up where we left off in October, as if we just saw one another the day before.

I'm not going to say it is easy to get back into the swing of things. It is hard when the baseball season is over—I don't know what to do with myself when there are no games to play. But just when I get used to my winter routine, suddenly it's the middle of February, and I wake up and have no idea where I'm headed. It's a little disorienting. Even though I've been looking forward to getting back on schedule, I still have to find a way to motivate myself and get ready for the new season. It usually takes me a couple of weeks to snap back into the regular-season routine, but once I do, the adrenaline rush kicks in a bit.

As much as I'd like to continue to sleep late and rest up for the regular season, I know how important spring training is—both physically and mentally. Everything we do during spring training gets us in shape and warmed up for the long season ahead. Every lap I run, every drill I do, every weight I lift gets me closer to another World Series ring. Just because we are doing drills in spring training and not during the regular season doesn't imply the exercises mean less—in fact, they mean more. The workout sessions are sharpening us physically and mentally as we start to prepare for the preseason games, and then opening day and beyond.

When I have time, I try to attend Little League games in Tampa with Tino.
His son plays, and we have a good time watching the kids.

About 60 guys show up for spring training. We have a 40-man roster: 25 whom we carry and then the rest who can be called up from the minors during the year. So there are around 20 guys who are trying out for a place on the team. You might think that there's a lot of pressure on us when training starts. Even though we have won three championships in a row, I don't think of it as pressure. It's more automatic than that—we just expect to do well, we expect to meet our goals as a team. What we need to do to achieve these goals is give each spring-training practice and exhibition game our absolute best effort.

The atmosphere is actually pretty relaxed. Although our manager

Joe Torre, keeps the mood very light, he also expects each of us to get ready individually and for us as a group to know what it's going to take to prepare properly for the season ahead. We have a lot of veterans on our team, so we don't really need to have instruction all of the time. But Mr. Torre trusts us to know what we need to do to get in shape, and he's always there to guide us. It's a bit of a relief for me when the players and Mr. Torre show up in Tampa. I lift weights and work out in the off-season pretty much by myself, but I really need to get out on the field with my teammates and practice hard in order to get back into the base-ball groove. When all of us are participating in the same drills at the

same time, taking batting practice, fielding ground balls, and that kind of thing, I can't help but get excited about taking the field in the first week of April.

The most difficult thing about spring training is running and getting your legs in shape. It's really an essential part of preparing for the rigorous and lengthy regular-season games that are around the corner. To be honest, the conditioning and agility workouts are my least favorite. But they don't seem to bother Bernie Williams, who's probably the best long-distance runner on the team. He used to run track when he was younger. Nevertheless, whether you excel at running, like Bernie, or dislike it like

I do, you've got to do every exercise at 100 percent. No excuses. If you don't, you're going to have a season filled with mistakes and errors that you could have avoided if you had only worked to the best of your ability.

Baseball is really in the air in Tampa, you can just feel it all around you. Game day is on the horizon. Sometimes I go to Little League games after practice is over. Tino Martinez's son plays, and I'll go with Tino to watch him. I get a kick out of seeing kids play because they really have fun. It always reminds me what's at the heart of the game. They love being out there, just as I loved it. Sharing in their joy helps keep me grounded and prepares me for the season.

I treat every spring training like it's my first ever and that I'm trying to make the Yankees all over again. I don't care that I've been the starting shortstop for five years, or that I was MVP of the World Series in 2000. Sure, I am going to have a good time in Tampa and have fun preparing for the season, but I am going to work like I have to earn my job, **because I do**.

THE MEDIA STARTS SHOWING UP IN TAMPA even before

some of the players do. The local New York stations send down

TV reporters, and there are plenty of journalists around. I'm

pretty used to the attention because in New York the cameras

are on you **constantly.** That's part of what players for New

York teams have to contend with on a regular basis, but it's

worth it to play in **NEW YORK.**

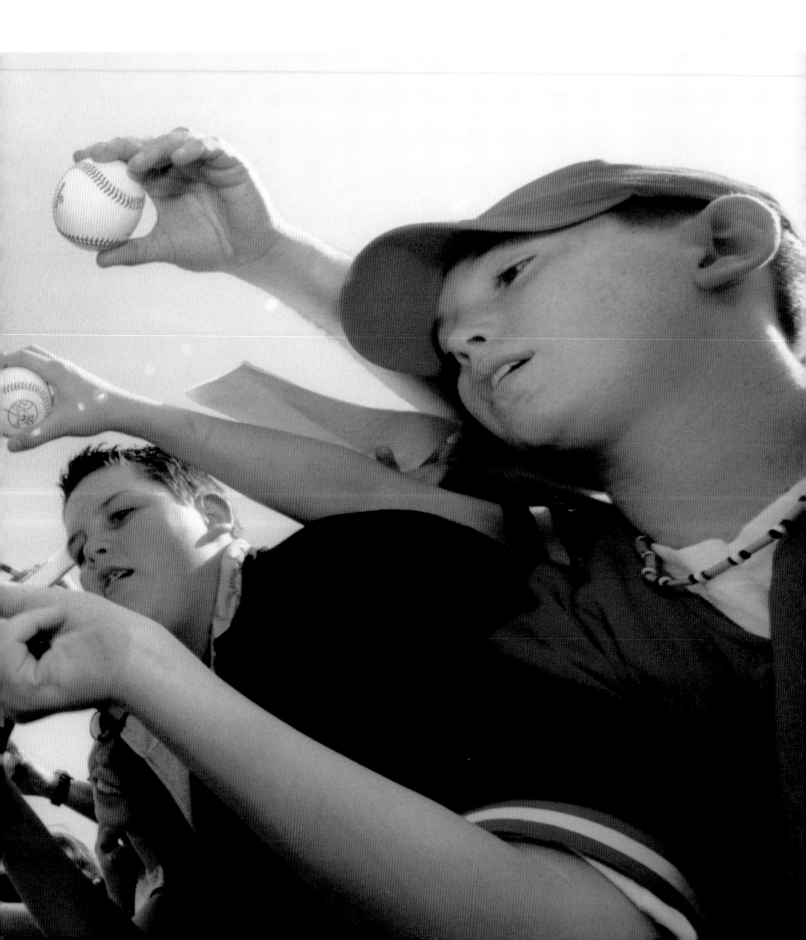

During spring training, **the fans** have a chance to get a lot closer to you than they do during the regular season. So I try to sign as much as I can to show how much I appreciate their support. Sometimes I will get a moment to **talk to a few of them,** and they will ask me questions about last season or the one coming up. It's always nice to hear their thoughts and their generous praise.

ONE OF THE PITCHING COACHES, BILLY CONNORS, opened a restaurant not far from Legends Field. Tino and I were the first patrons—the food was actually excellent! During the regular season, **I go out with my teammates all of the time.** It's quieter in Tampa,

though. Tino lives down there, but everyone else is away until spring training, so **I don't see too many of the guys during the off-season.** I like to visit our catcher, Jorge Posada, in Puerto Rico a few times a year.

After spring-training practice and games, I go back to my place to **relax**. For a few years I lived in an apartment, and I really wanted to get a house. I finally found a great one—it's not huge, but it's **just right for me.** Gerald Williams, my good friend and former teammate, lives a few doors down from me, which is great for both of us. We're able to hang out, watch movies, that kind of thing. My home is where I feel the most **comfortable.**

My parents actually bought me this golf putter for Christmas because my golf game is nothing to brag about. They thought it would help me improve, but I don't think I'm getting any better! It's a sport that requires a lot of patience and skill. Unfortunately, when I play I usually end up hitting houses and cars. I think it's safe to say I won't be leaving baseball to join a PGA tour anytime soon.

PEOPLE MIGHT BE SURPRISED TO HEAR THAT I'M A REAL HOMEBODY. Fans may think I'm out partying every night, but that's not true. Other than going out to eat and to a movie, **I am home 90 percent of the time.** Tampa can be a fast-paced city if you want it to be, but I prefer to keep it quiet. Tampa is a nice change from New York because **it's so laid-back.** I look forward to going down there after the season is over. I am able to relax a little and get ready for the **long season ahead.**

FIELD OF DREAMS

After the Yankees won our fourth World Series title in five years in 2000, newspaper and TV reporters kept asking me how I was going to keep myself motivated now that we had achieved so much success as a team. They didn't understand that finding the motivation to win is the easy part. Take Yogi Berra, for instance. Yogi is a Yankee hero and New York legend. He's around the stadium sometimes throughout the year. Yogi has ten World Series rings. Ten! All you have to do is look at him and know that no matter how good you have it, here is a guy who has done better. True, I have a long way to go before I reach ten rings, but I believe it's a goal that is never out of my grasp.

Motivation never has been a problem for me. I have spent most of my life trying to get to where I am today—playing baseball year-round. Don't think I ever forget that. I have a job to do. I go to work with my teammates 162 days a year—at Yankee Stadium, Camden Yards, Fenway, and even at Shea. If we work hard and have a little bit of luck, I get to put in overtime in the postseason. I wish everyone could be so excited going to their jobs every day.

There are a few things that I have learned playing in the major leagues for the last six years. These lessons have gotten me through game days in April, when the temperature was freezing at night; hot, sticky game days in June, as the season approached the halfway point; and in August, where we'd be fighting down the homestretch to keep our place on top of the A.L. East and make it to the play-offs:

I.   The season is long. You can't live and die with one game. Whether you have a great at bat that breaks the tie in extra innings, or make a terrible error that leads the other team to victory, you have to stay on an even keel.

2. Never take a victory home with you. Cherish the triumph for a few moments, but remember that there's another game tomorrow that you need to win to get to the postseason.

3. Don't dwell on the losses. If you overthink what happened in a game you lost, you will drive yourself crazy. You have to learn to shrug off the errors and mistakes and learn from them.

It's also important to remember that baseball is a humbling sport. You can be on top of the world in one minute and at the bottom in the next. It's like that day to day. It's the only sport where you can go out and have five hits one day, and in the next outing you might strike out four times. The only thing I can do in the wake of that fact is keep asking myself, "What can I do today to get better as a player and a person?"

There's always another game day during the regular season, another new opportunity to get up, work out, drive to Yankee Stadium or wherever we are playing, warm up with the other players, and take my place on the field. There is always another team to beat. Because we are the New York Yankees and have won so many championships, other ball clubs are always gunning to defeat us. They are constantly playing their best and trying to come out here and rattle us. That's why we have to be ready every single day. The goal is to tap into that competitive spirit throughout each game. With Yogi and his ten rings around, it will be a long time before I can take it easy.

Center fielder Bernie Williams and I are having a little fun while we do our warmup stretches.

I PRETTY MUCH FOLLOW THE SAME ROUTINE EVERY GAME DAY: I wake up, watch some TV, work out, and get dressed. Nothing too exciting. Every few weeks I'll get my hair cut—my friend Mike Daddy comes over to my apartment to do it. That's about as thrilling as my day gets before I head to the stadium. I think it's good to stick to a routine, though—it helps keep me focused on what really counts (the game).

I LIVE BY MYSELF, SO I TAKE CARE OF A LOT OF THINGS ON MY OWN. I do my own ironing and pick up my dry cleaning, just like **everyone** else. Some people may think because I have a high-profile job that I might be out of touch with the real world, but that's just not the case. If I don't do these things, they won't get done!

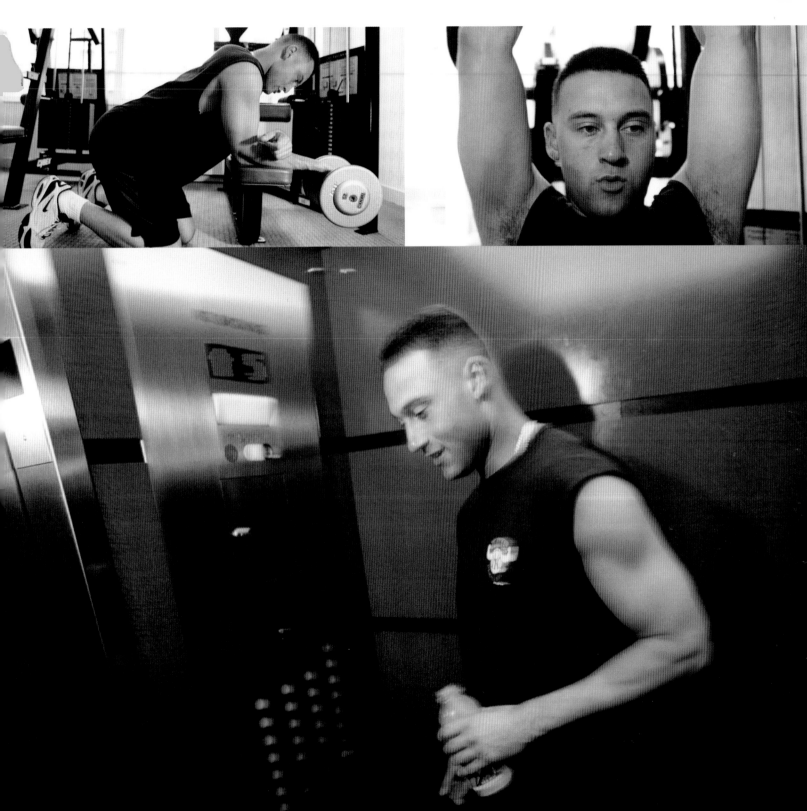

MY WORKOUT REGIMEN ON GAME DAY ISN'T TOO STRENUOUS, just **30** minutes or so. **I** like to exercise in the **morning,** so I get it out of the way before I go to the stadium. My apartment building has a gym, so I don't have any excuses for not working out.

FANS SEND MAIL TO THE STADIUM, AND IT GETS FORWARDED TO MY APARTMENT.
I used to be able to handle it all myself, but as you can see by these thick stacks of
letters, I need some help getting back to everyone now.

THE STREETS OF NEW YORK ARE FILLED WITH YANKEE FANS WHO STOP ME AND say hello. I love New York. I love the diversity and the fact that you can do just about anything or go anywhere. If you **crave pizza at three in the morning**, you can find a

place close by that's open for business. **My friend Sean Twitty** (or "Twit," as I call him) and I are walking down the street here, looking for a place to eat lunch before I drive to the stadium. **Most days I drive my own car to the Bronx. Here I am threading my way through Manhattan** traffic.

HITTING BALLS OFF THE TEE IS AN IMPORTANT PART OF WARMING UP BEFORE a game. I don't fool around. I imagine that I am hitting off David Wells or Pedro Martinez when I swing through, **smacking** the ball to the right, center, and left. It can be a little monotonous practicing my swing over and over again, but **it pays off in the long run.** If it helps me get good at bats against Martinez, Wells, and the other pitchers, then I'll swing all day.

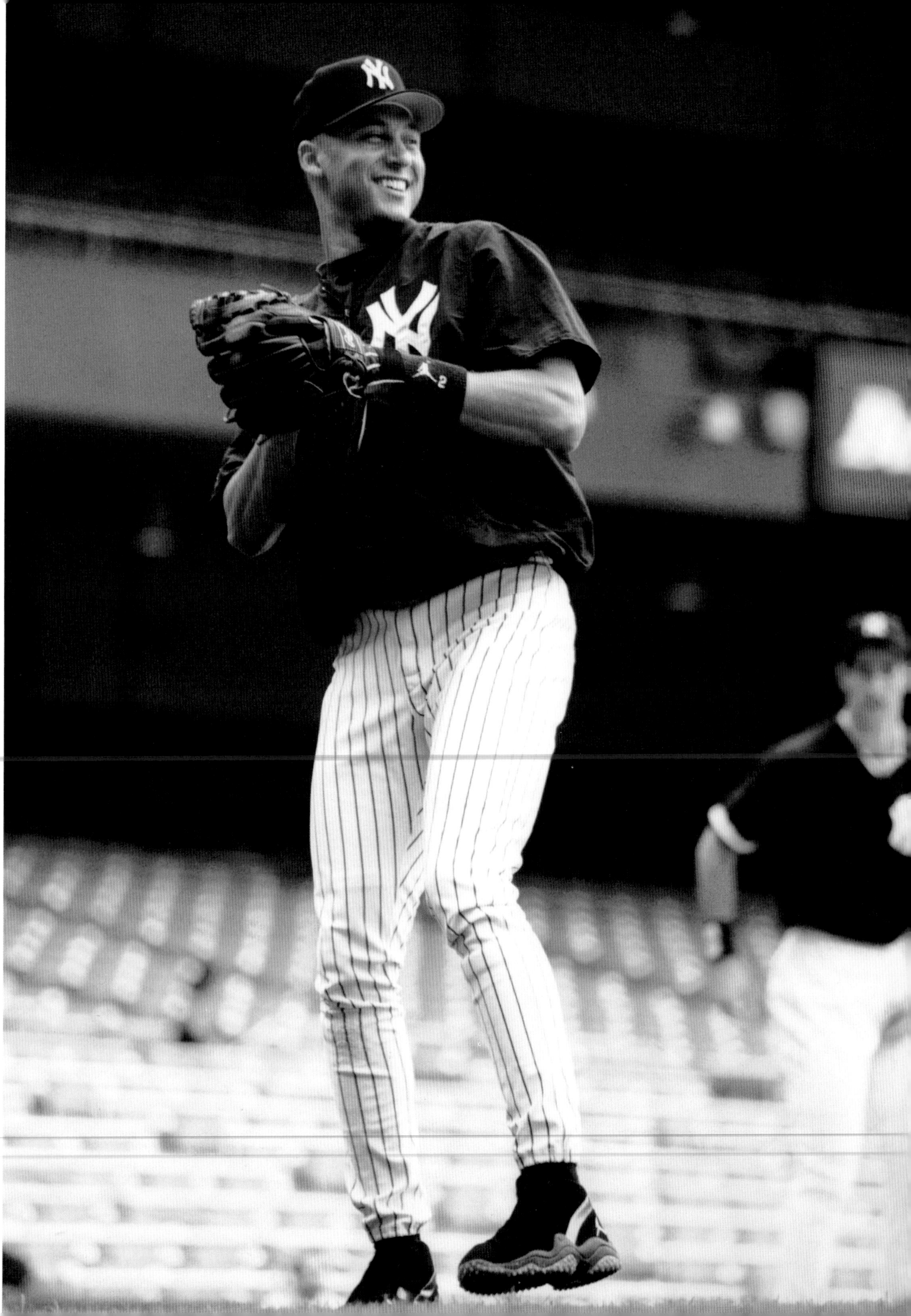

I WILL KID AROUND WHEN WE WARM UP AND CRACK JOKES WITH THE OTHER PLAYERS, BUT I REALLY DO TAKE OUR WARMUP SERIOUSLY. The practice throws and swings on game day guard us against injuries that could end the year for any

one of us. We stretch to make sure our muscles aren't tight, and we take batting practice and throw to loosen up our arms and joints. **ALL OF THIS IS ESSENTIAL TO PREPARE FOR THE UPCOMING GAME.**

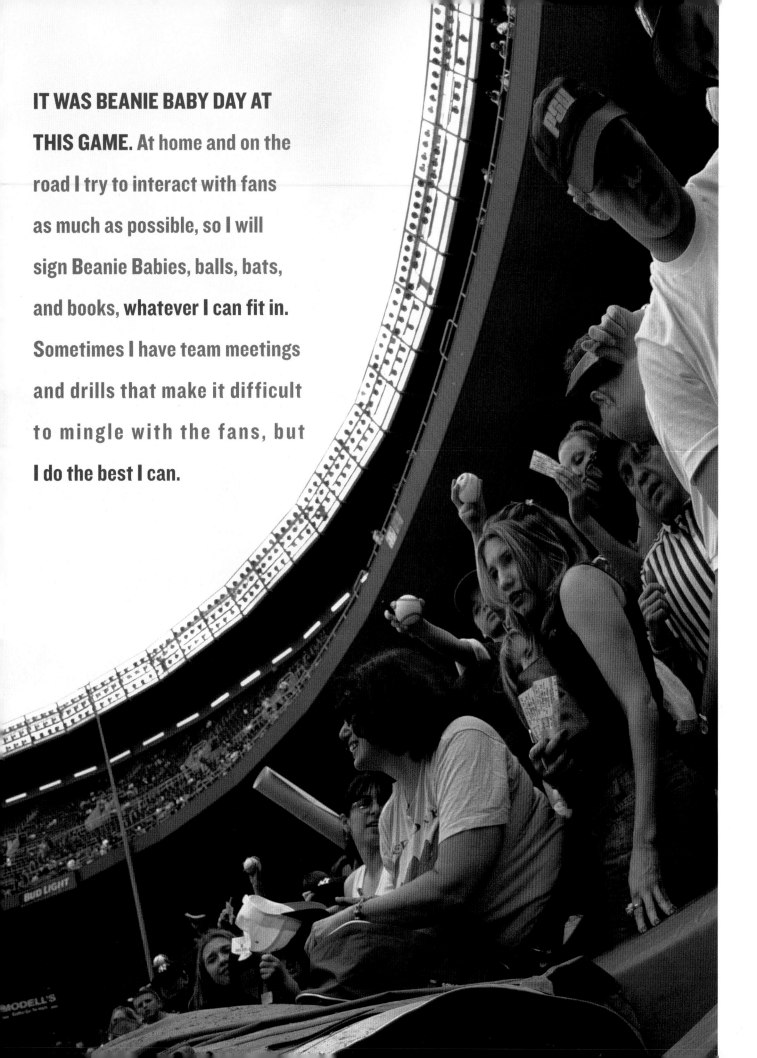

IT WAS BEANIE BABY DAY AT THIS GAME. At home and on the road I try to interact with fans as much as possible, so I will sign Beanie Babies, balls, bats, and books, **whatever I can fit in.** Sometimes I have team meetings and drills that make it difficult to mingle with the fans, but **I do the best I can.**

GAME
D·A·Y
ADMIT ONE

I DON'T WORRY ABOUT MY STATISTICS. I try to hit the ball hard or with more authority at any given time, but I don't sit around and focus on my numbers of home runs or doubles or RBIs. The minute

ou do that, you start to forget what's important. The object is to win ball games. **I will help my team do that any way I can.**

I'M NOT PERFECT. I have made errors that have caused us to lose games. I have dropped balls, struck out with men on base, been caught stealing to end a rally. The best players fail at times. But I look at all the balls I catch, not the ones I miss, and I savor the game-winning hits and try not to worry about the strikeouts. The second after we lose a game, I tell myself to forget it. I'll just get them next time.

WHEN YOU ARE PLAYING IN TIGHT GAMES, anything can happen. If you get a cheap hit or run hard or make a double play or steal a base, you can change the

whole direction of the game. That's why it is **so important to focus on the little things,** because it's **the little things** that turn a game around.

I PRESENTED YOGI BERRA'S WIFE WITH FLOWERS ON YOGI BERRA DAY. The Yankees are spoiled because we have a lot of former players who come back to visit. We are able to recognize them for their unbelievable careers with the Yankees. In 2001, we are having one for Dave Winfield, whom I have admired since I was a child. I started the Turn 2 Foundation for kids who are at risk of substance abuse because Dave had started his own nonprofit organization years ago. I was really inspired by what he did.

I WOULD TAKE THE CHANCE TO BE THE HERO OR THE GOAT IN EVERY GAME I PLAY FOR THE REST OF MY LIFE. Those moments are what make playing sports so exhilarating, whether it's a last-second shot, a field goal as time expires, or a 3-2 count with two outs and the winning run on base in the ninth inning. I love being in those situations with the Yankees, those tense moments during the regular season as we chase another title. TO ME, THAT'S FUN.

DURING THE GAME, MY MIND IS NEVER AT REST. I concentrate on every aspect of the game. Since I'm the shortstop, I have to keep up my end on the defensive side. At the same time, I've got to step up to the plate and see the ways in which I can advance a runner. My mental focus has to be flexible enough that I can stay levelheaded and watch everything that is happening around my teammates and me as well.

THERE'S JUST NO PLACE LIKE HOME. I've played all over, and I like a lot of the stadiums. Seattle's is very modern, and Baltimore and Cleveland have great facilities, too. But none of them can compare to Yankee Stadium. There's so much tradition within those walls, and I'm always aware of how **lucky I am** to be able to go there every day and play for the **greatest team** in baseball history. I think about that every game day when I enter the stadium and when I leave. It's an awesome responsibility, **BUT I AM UP TO THE CHALLENGE.**

GLORY DAYS

The 2000 World Series games were the most thrilling games I've ever played, better than my first World Series, better than the Series the year we won 125 games. All of New York was involved, and the excitement surrounding the city was amazing. I don't know what it was like in the rest of the country, but you couldn't get away from the enthusiasm here, and I didn't want to. I think it was fun for everyone, especially Yankee fans, of course. However, none of us got any sleep for those days. The games were so late, and when your adrenaline is flowing after a tight game, you can't really fall asleep. Then you've got to get up early and do it all over again. So in some strange way, it almost seemed like one long day to me.

During the regular season, I really concentrate on getting to the moment where every at bat and play matters, where every game is on the line. Those 30 exhibition games in the spring and 162 regular-season games don't mean a thing if we don't get the ring. It doesn't make a difference that we won the World Series in 1996, 1998, and 1999. I want to win it again and again.

I approach a game day in the postseason the same way I do during the regular season. The preparation is exactly alike. What I do during the daytime, how I work out and warm up at the stadium, doesn't really change. There is a lot I have to try and ignore, though. There is more media hype surrounding the play-offs and especially the World Series. There are cameras everywhere you turn and large groups of reporters asking you for interviews. The season is on the line, too, whether it is the first game of the American League Championships or the World Series. But I don't let any of that get to me. I just continue to go about things at my own pace and keep my focus as sharp as I would during the regular season.

I hugged my sister, Sharlee, after we won the 2000 World Series.

Despite the intense crowds and cameras catching your every move, one place where we can relax as a team is in the locker room. The media isn't allowed to hang around before the game like they do during the regular season. They can get in only after we have played. In a way, it helps the team loosen up more in the clubhouse. We get to talk with one another more candidly and also take time out for ourselves so that we can mentally prepare for the big innings ahead.

There are so many reasons that we've made it to the postseason five years in a row and have won the World Series four times. Still, there has been one constant factor in all those journeys. There is a lot you can say about a team just by looking at their manager. Joe Torre happens to be the best in the majors. Everyone loves him and wants to do right by him. During the season he keeps things together and runs the organization smoothly. He's a player's manager—he doesn't get on you unless he needs to, and he would never embarrass you. I've learned so much from him about considerate behavior and leadership. Mr. Torre never panics, and he always stays positive. That's why the Yankees continue to play great, confident baseball, and why we continue to make it to the postseason. Mr. Torre is really calm during the year, but when we win the Series, he gets pretty emotional. He doesn't need to say much to

The 2000 World Series was really something special, though. Going into Shea Stadium during the Series wasn't anything like walking on the field during interleague play. Even though we had been to the Series many times before, the intensity level at Shea was unbelievable. This was definitely a must-win situation for our team, even more than in any other Series game any other year. There was a real sense of urgency. The Mets had a great team, and all of the matchups were close. In fact, a few, if not all, of the games could have gone either way. And we wanted to win it—the sooner the better—even if it meant having to take the championship at Shea.

Winning the MVP award after we had prevailed in Game 5 was really an added bonus, and also an incredible honor. Players don't ever think about being named MVP. Basically, our goal is to get through the season successfully, make it to the postseason, play in the World Series, and win. So being given the MVP trophy was something that had never crossed my mind. When they announced I had won it, I was thrilled, but at the same time I felt like they could have given it to anyone. We had a lot of guys who played well and contributed to our victory. Actually, I feel as though I'm just the person they chose to hold it for

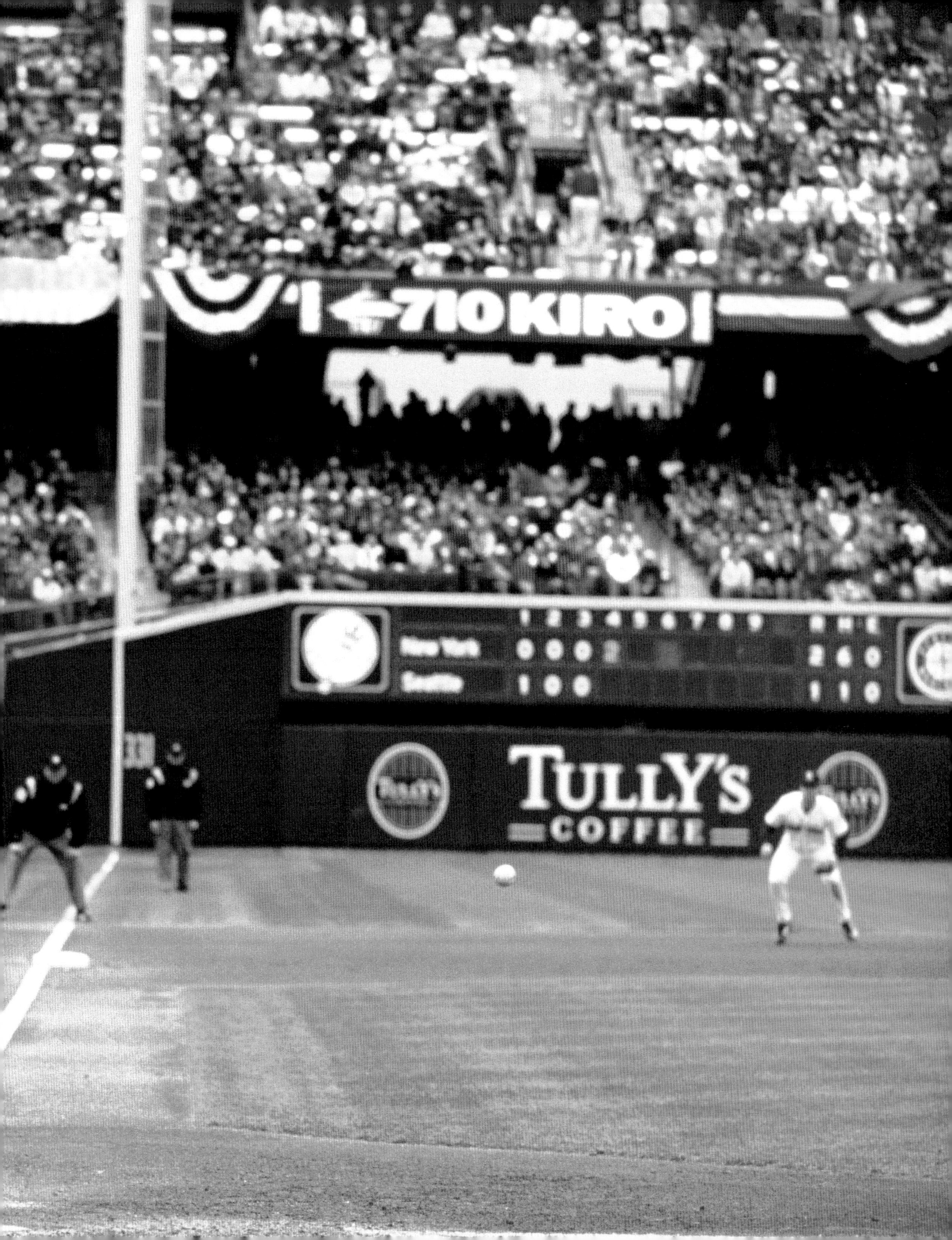
710 KIRO
New York
Seattle
TULLY'S
COFFEE

The fans are so **passionate** during the postseason—even the ones who are cheering on the opposing team. No matter if we're on the road or playing at home, I like to see the fans get **into the game**, including the people who aren't behind the Yankees. I just want everyone in the stands to get excited about baseball **like I do.**

I TRY NOT TO CHANGE ANYTHING DURING THE POSTSEASON, not how I play the game or how much I concentrate on my offense or defense. I keep it simple, treat these games like they are part of the regular season. I wouldn't say I try harder, because that kind of insinuates that I don't give it my all during the rest of the year, which isn't true. I do have more butterflies, though. Nevertheless, I get out there and put myself on the line, whether it's the 60th game of the regular season or Game 7 of the World Series. That's the kind of attitude that breeds SUCCESS.

I DON'T GO OUT AND TRY TO HIT HOME RUNS IN THE POSTSEASON, but obviously it's a great feeling when I can contribute with **big hits** like those. Everyone wants to play well during the play-offs because all eyes are on you, particularly when you make it to the World Series. Whether you're a baseball fan, or a sportswriter, or a television journalist covering baseball, there are no other games to watch. In a sense, when **all the attention** is being directed at you, you want to come through for your team and show everyone **what you've got.**

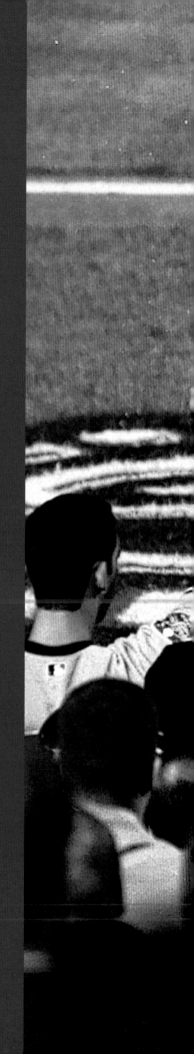

IT IS SUCH A GREAT FEELING TO CONTRIB- UTE IN THE PLAY- OFFS. I start working out in November, then get together with the team in Tampa, and play with them through a long season. We have worked so hard together for one pur- pose—to win. That's really all that matters. I have always looked at the game that way. There's no use playing if you aren't trying to take it all. Baseball, board games, JEOP- ARDY! on TV, it doesn't matter to me. **I HATE TO LOSE.**

WHEN WE STARTED THE SEASON, I DON'T THINK ANY OF US COULD HAVE predicted that it was going to end with a showdown between the Yankees and the Mets. There was a lot of talk, though, before we got to the play-offs, because **in 1999 the Mets were so close** to making it to the World Series, but then the Braves got the best of them in the postseason. Sportscasters were suspecting that there might be a

Yankees-Mets matchup in the championships, and it stirred up a lot of excitement in the fans because we have a little **hometown rivalry going on.** When it finally became a reality, we had to try to get past all the hype, settle down, and focus on winning because the Mets weren't going to hand us the championship. **THEY WANTED THIS AS BADLY AS WE DID.**

WE HAD A LOT ON THE LINE AGAINST THE METS. We would have had to pack up and leave Manhattan if we had lost to them. Our three championships wouldn't have been worth much. Imagining the Mets in the victory parade kept us focused on **winning the series.**

MY DAD, MOM, AND SISTER **ARE THE FIRST PEOPLE I LOOK FOR AFTER WE** win. I have been really fortunate—my parents have been able to attend all of the World Series games throughout the years, and my sister, Sharlee, saw all but San Diego in 1999 when we won. It's so wonderful to have my family there

to cheer me on. They know what my dreams have been, and they've seen me through the whole journey—from my Little League and high-school days to the major leagues. I have always had my family's support, and that's why I want to share our victories with them first.

THERE ARE SO MANY EMOTIONS RUNNING THROUGH YOU AFTER YOU WIN A GAME LIKE
Game 5 in the Series, but there aren't too many words that can be said. You can just tell
from your teammates' eyes that everyone feels the same way—exhilarated. All of your hard

work has paid off, and you made it there with your team, the people you see more than your families. We spend a lot of our time together, and when we win, it's really a feeling that's difficult to describe. **IT'S A SENSATION UNLIKE ANY OTHER.**

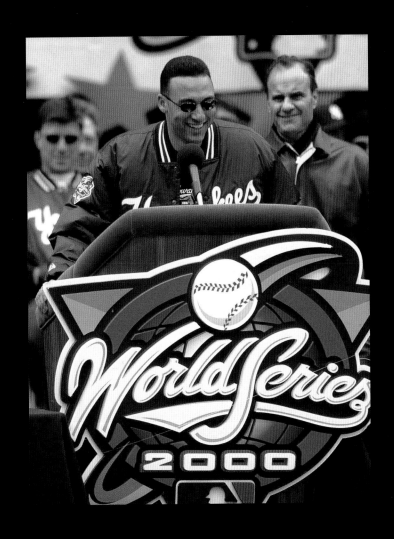

EVERY YEAR THAT WE ARE IN THE WORLD SERIES FEELS A BIT DIFFERENT, but I have to say that 2000 meant a little bit more to me. This season was special because a Subway Series hadn't happened in more than 40 years and because New York City was really in an uproar. It's hard to think how we are going to top 2000. Are we going to become the first team in almost 50 years to win four championships in a row? Who knows? But no matter what happens, I know that eventually we will find a way to **surprise** people.

Photo Credits

4–5

Jonathan Daniel/
SPORTS ILLUSTRATED

8

Spring Training; Tampa, FL
February 20, 2001
© Walter Iooss, Jr.

12

Spring Training; Tampa, FL
February 20, 2001
© Walter Iooss, Jr.

12

Spring Training; Tampa, FL
February 20, 2001
© Walter Iooss, Jr.

12

Spring Training; Tampa, FL
February 20, 2001
© Walter Iooss, Jr.

12

Spring Training; Tampa, FL
February 20, 2001
© Walter Iooss, Jr.

12

Spring Training; Tampa, FL
February 20, 2001
© Walter Iooss, Jr.

12

Spring Training; Tampa, FL
February 20, 2001
© Walter Iooss, Jr.

13

Spring Training; Tampa, FL
February 20, 2001
© Walter Iooss, Jr.

14

Spring Training; Tampa, FL
February 20, 2001
© Walter Iooss, Jr.

16

Spring Training; Tampa, FL
February 20, 2001
© Walter Iooss, Jr.

17

Spring Training; Tampa, FL
February 20, 2001
© Walter Iooss, Jr.

18–19

Spring Training; Tampa, FL
February 20, 2001
© Walter Iooss, Jr.

20

Spring Training; Tampa, FL
February 20, 2001
© Walter Iooss, Jr.

20

Spring Training; Tampa, FL
February 20, 2001
© Walter Iooss, Jr.

21

Spring Training; Tampa, FL
February 20, 2001
© Walter Iooss, Jr.

22

Spring Training; Tampa, FL
February 20, 2001
© Walter Iooss, Jr.

23

Spring Training; Tampa, FL
February 20, 2001
© Walter Iooss, Jr.

24–25

Spring Training; Tampa, FL
February 20, 2001
© Walter Iooss, Jr.

26

Spring Training; Tampa, FL
February 20, 2001
© Walter Iooss, Jr.

26

Spring Training; Tampa, FL
February 20, 2001
© Walter Iooss, Jr.

27

Spring Training; Tampa, FL
February 20, 2001
© Walter Iooss, Jr.

28

Spring Training; Tampa, FL
February 20, 2001
© Walter Iooss, Jr.

29

Spring Training; Tampa, FL
February 20, 2001
© Walter Iooss, Jr.

29

Spring Training; Tampa, FL
February 20, 2001
© Walter Iooss, Jr.

30

Spring Training; Tampa, FL
February 20, 2001
© Walter Iooss, Jr.

31

Spring Training; Tampa, FL
February 20, 2001
© Walter Iooss, Jr.

32

Spring Training; Tampa, FL
February 20, 2001
© Walter Iooss, Jr.

33

Spring Training; Tampa, FL
February 20, 2001
© Walter Iooss, Jr.

34–35

Spring Training; Tampa, FL
February 20, 2001
© Walter Iooss, Jr.

36

Chuck Solomon/
SPORTS ILLUSTRATED

38

August 4, 2000
© Walter Iooss, Jr.

38

August 4, 2000
© Walter Iooss, Jr.

39

August 4, 2000
© Walter Iooss, Jr.

40–41

Chuck Solomon/
SPORTS ILLUSTRATED

42

August 4, 2000
© Walter Iooss, Jr.

42

August 4, 2000
© Walter Iooss, Jr.

42

August 4, 2000
© Walter Iooss, Jr.

42

August 4, 2000
© Walter Iooss, Jr.

43

August 4, 2000
© Walter Iooss, Jr.

44

August 4, 2000
© Walter Iooss, Jr.

45

August 4, 2000
© Walter Iooss, Jr.

45

August 4, 2000
© Walter Iooss, Jr.

45

August 4, 2000
© Walter Iooss, Jr.

45

August 4, 2000
© Walter Iooss, Jr.

46

August 4, 2000
© Walter Iooss, Jr.

46

August 4, 2000
© Walter Iooss, Jr.

46

August 4, 2000
© Walter Iooss, Jr.

47

August 4, 2000
© Walter Iooss, Jr.

47

August 4, 2000
© Walter Iooss, Jr.

47

August 4, 2000
© Walter Iooss, Jr.

48

August 4, 2000
© Walter Iooss, Jr.

49

August 4, 2000
© Walter Iooss, Jr.

50

August 4, 2000
© Walter Iooss, Jr.

51

August 4, 2000
© Walter Iooss, Jr.

52

August 4, 2000
© Walter Iooss, Jr.

53

August 4, 2000
© Walter Iooss, Jr.

54

August 4, 2000
© Walter Iooss, Jr.

55

August 4, 2000
© Walter Iooss, Jr.

55

August 4, 2000
© Walter Iooss, Jr.

56–57

© Rob Tringali Jr.
SPORTSCHROME USA

58

Stephen Green/
SPORTS ILLUSTRATED

59

Stephen Green/
SPORTS ILLUSTRATED

60–61

© Rob Tringali Jr.
SPORTSCHROME USA

62

August 4, 2000
© Walter Iooss, Jr.

63

Chuck Solomon/
SPORTS ILLUSTRATED

64

Al Tielemans/
SPORTS ILLUSTRATED

65

October 24, 2000
World Series
Yankees (2) at Mets (4)
Ezra Shaw/ALLSPORT

66–67

Stephen Green/
SPORTS ILLUSTRATED

68–69

July 18, 1999
Expos (0) at Yankees (6)
Vincent LaForet
ALLSPORT

70

May 27, 2000
Red Sox vs Yankees
© Rob Tringali Jr.
SPORTSCHROME USA

70

April 30, 2000
Blue Jays at Yanks
© Rob Tringali Jr.
SPORTSCHROME USA

70
August 28, 1999
Mariners (I) at Yankees (2)
M. David Leeds/ALLSPORT

70
September 2, 1999
Oakland A's (3) at Yankees (9)
Ezra Shaw/ALLSPORT

70
May 27, 2000
Red Sox vs. Yanks
© Rob Tringali Jr.
SPORTSCHROME USA

71
August 4, 1999
Blue Jays (3) at Yankees (8)
Ezra Shaw/ALLSPORT

72-73
August 4, 1999
Blue Jays (3) at Yankees (8)
Ezra Shaw/ALLSPORT

74
August 4, 1999
Blue Jays (3) at Yankees (8)
Ezra Shaw/ALLSPORT

75
May 8, 1999
Mariners (14) at Yankees (5)
Ezra Shaw/ALLSPORT

76
June 5, 1999
Mets (3) at Yankees (6)
David Leeds/ALLSPORT

77
May 29, 2000
Oakland A's vs. Yankees
© Rob Tringali Jr.
SPORTSCHROME USA

78-79
October 13, 1999
Red Sox (3) at Yankees (4)
Jamie Squire/ALLSPORT

80
© Walter Iooss, Jr/
SPORTS ILLUSTRATED

82
World Series Game 5
Yankees (3) vs. Mets (2)
© Rob Tringali Jr.
SPORTSCHROME USA

83
World Series Game 5
Yankees (3) vs. Mets (2)
© Rob Tringali Jr.
SPORTSCHROME USA

84-85
Chuck Solomon/
SPORTS ILLUSTRATED

86
Chuck Solomon/
SPORTS ILLUSTRATED

87
Robert Beck/
SPORTS ILLUSTRATED

88
Robert Beck/
SPORTS ILLUSTRATED

88
Robert Beck/
SPORTS ILLUSTRATED

88
Robert Beck/
SPORTS ILLUSTRATED

89
V.J. Lovero/
SPORTS ILLUSTRATED

91
Manny Millan/
SPORTS ILLUSTRATED

92-93
Al Tielemans/
SPORTS ILLUSTRATED

94
2000 World Series
Yankees vs Mets
© Rob Tringali Jr.
SPORTSCHROME USA

95
2000 World Series
Yankees vs Mets
© Rob Tringali Jr.
SPORTSCHROME USA

96

2000 World Series, Game 5
Yankees vs Mets
© Rob Tringali Jr.
SPORTSCHROME USA

105

David Leeds
ALLSPORT

97

October 24, 2000
World Series
Yankees (2) at Mets (4)
Ezra Shaw
ALLSPORT

98–99

2000 World Series, Game 5
Yankees vs Mets
© Rob Tringali Jr.
SPORTSCHROME USA

100

© Walter Iooss, Jr/
SPORTS ILLUSTRATED

101

© Walter Iooss, Jr/
SPORTS ILLUSTRATED

101

© Walter Iooss, Jr/
SPORTS ILLUSTRATED

102–103

2000 World Series, Game 5
Yankees vs Mets
© Rob Tringali Jr.
SPORTSCHROME USA

104

Al Bello
ALLSPORT